Fishing in the Coorong

By Emma Scarce

Library For All Ltd.

Fishing in the Coorong

First published 2023

Published by Library For All Ltd
Email: info@libraryforall.org
URL: libraryforall.org

Our Yarning logo design by Jason Lee, Bidjipidji Art

Original illustrations by Caitlyn McPherson

Fishing in the Coorong
Scarce, Emma
ISBN: 978-1-922991-08-9
SKU03437

Fishing in the Coorong

We respect and honour Aboriginal and Torres Strait Islander Elders past, present and future. We acknowledge the stories, traditions and living cultures of Aboriginal and Torres Strait Islander peoples on this land and commit to building a brighter future together.

I love the Coorong. The air is fresh.

It's Ngarrindjerri Country, where my nanna lives.

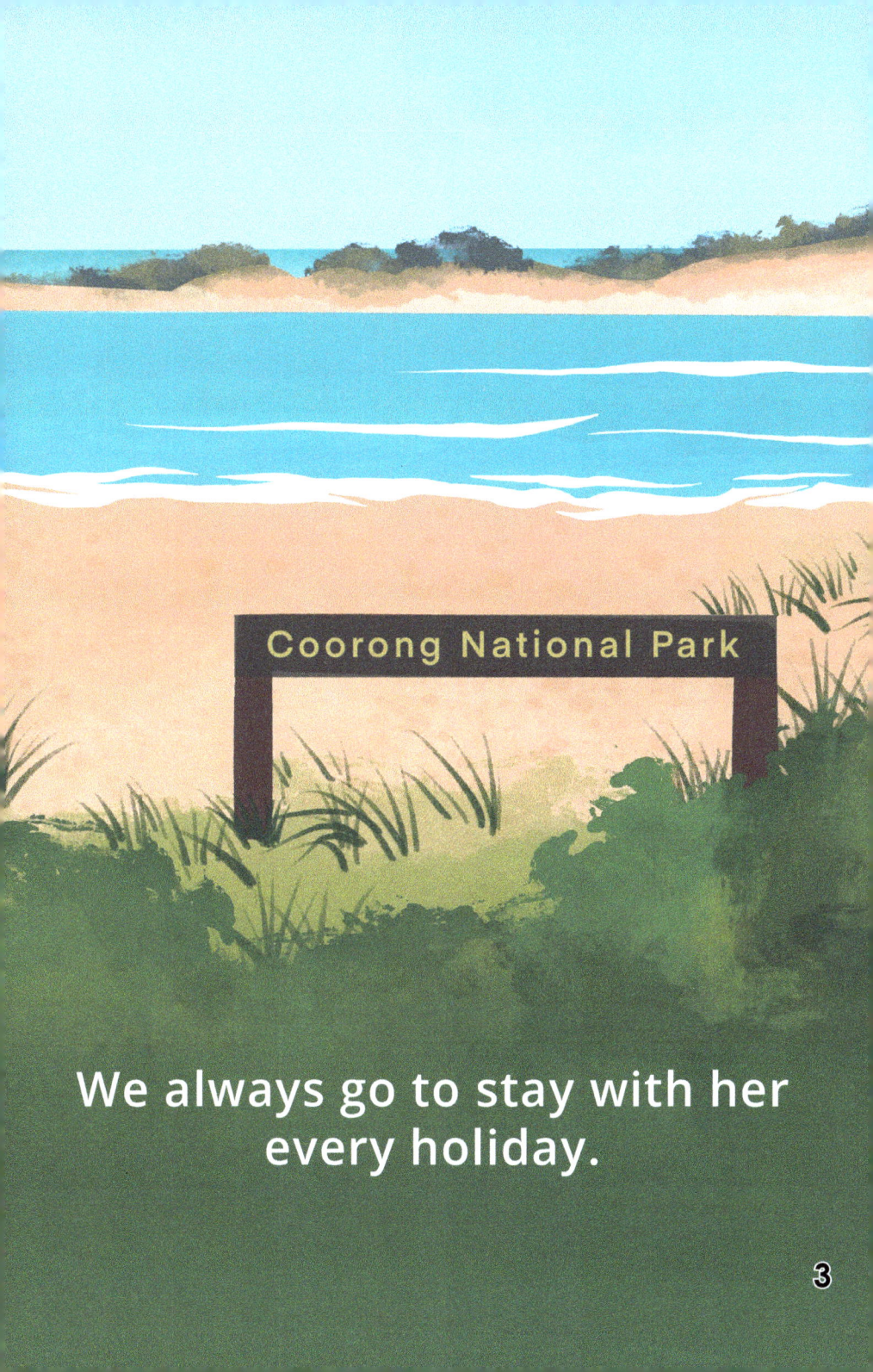

Coorong National Park

We always go to stay with her every holiday.

One day, I went with Nanna down to the water to catch some fish for dinner.

We were chatting away when we spotted a pelican who was hurt.

He was stuck by the water.

Nanna grabbed a towel and covered him gently, then carried him home.

Nanna tied up the pelican's sore wing and we made up a bed in the laundry for him.

We shared some of our fish with him, too.

Nanna said he will heal quickly if he rests and eats.

We played music to keep him calm.

Over the next week, Nanna and I caught fish for the pelican.

He drank water and he rested.

One day he put his head up.
He looked better.

Nanna said he was healed,
and we could take him back
to the beach.

When we put him by the water, another pelican called to our friend, and they swam away together.

Nanna and I were very happy.

You can use these questions to talk about this book with your family, friends and teachers.

What did you learn from this book?

Describe this book in one word. Funny? Scary? Colourful? Interesting?

How did this book make you feel when you finished reading it?

What was your favourite part of this book?

About the author

Emma is from the Karuna, Ngarrindjeri and Mirning
Nations and lives in Adelaide on Karuna Country.
She loves a good story and laughs with her family.
Emma liked *Banana's in Pajamas* when she was little.

Our Yarning

Want to discover more books from this collection? Our Yarning is a collection of books written by Aboriginal and Torres Strait Islander peoples across Australia.

We know that children learn better, and enjoy reading more, when they see themselves in the stories, characters and illustrations of the books they read.

To download the app, visit the Google Play Store on any Android device and search 'Our Yarning'.

libraryforall.org